Commercial Lending Made Simple
A Guide to Financial Products and Definitions

Malcolm Holden

Disclaimer

The information provided in this book on financial products and investing is intended for general informational purposes only and should not be considered as professional financial advice. The content is based on the knowledge available up to the publication date and may not reflect the most current market conditions or regulatory changes.

Investing in financial products carries inherent risks, and readers are urged to conduct their due diligence and seek advice from qualified financial advisors before making any investment decisions. The author, publisher, and any affiliated parties do not assume any responsibility or liability for the accuracy, completeness, or applicability of the information presented in this book.

Furthermore, past performance of any financial product is not indicative of future results. The performance of investments can fluctuate, and there is no guarantee that any strategy or approach will yield positive outcomes.

Readers should be aware that investing involves potential loss of principal, and they are advised to consider their risk tolerance and financial goals carefully before investing in any financial product mentioned in this book.

The author and publisher do not endorse or recommend any specific financial products, companies, or investment strategies mentioned in this book. The inclusion of such information is for illustrative purposes only and should not be construed as a solicitation or recommendation to buy or sell any financial product.

By reading this book, readers acknowledge and agree that the author and publisher are not liable for any direct or indirect damages, losses, or expenses arising from the use or misuse of the information provided herein.

Always consult with qualified professionals, such as financial advisors, tax consultants, and legal experts, before implementing any financial strategies or making investment decisions.

In conclusion, this book is not a substitute for professional financial advice, and readers are encouraged to seek individualized guidance to address their specific financial situations and needs.

Commercial Lending Made Simple

TABLE OF CONTENTS

FORWARD

I wrote this book to help people unfamiliar with the commercial lending process gain a better understanding of their available options as well as help them grow their knowledge on the subject.

Chapter 1: Introduction to Commercial Lending

Commercial lending is a critical component of the financial industry that provides businesses with access to capital. It allows businesses to expand, hire employees, purchase inventory, and invest in their future growth. Commercial lending is also a key driver of the economy, as it helps businesses create jobs and drive economic growth.

Commercial lending is the process of providing loans to businesses. These loans are typically used to finance working capital, purchase equipment, or invest in real estate. Commercial loans are offered by banks, credit unions, and other financial institutions.

These commercial loans can come in two forms: secured and unsecured. Secured loans require collateral, which is an asset that is pledged as security for the loan. This collateral can be anything of value, such as equipment, inventory, trust accounts, assets, or real estate. Unsecured loans on the other hand do not require collateral, but they typically have higher interest rates and stricter repayment terms.

The commercial lending process is complex and involves a variety of variables. The first step in the process is determining the borrower's creditworthiness. This involves reviewing the borrower's credit history, financial statements, and tax returns. Next, the lender will look at the borrower's debt-to-income ratio and other financial metrics to determine whether the borrower is a good credit risk.

Once the lender has determined the borrower's creditworthiness, they can determine the loan rate and terms. There are many other factors that go into this decision including, the purpose of the loan, the borrower's financial situation, and the lender's risk tolerance. The lender will also consider the interest rate, repayment term, and collateral requirements for the loan.

Commercial lending can be a complex and intimidating process for many business owners and those unfamiliar with the process. However, by understanding the basics of the commercial lending process, borrowers can make informed decisions about their financing needs. The key to success in borrowing money is to have a solid business plan and a clear understanding of the financial metrics that lenders use to evaluate creditworthiness.

In conclusion, commercial lending is a critical component of the financial industry that provides businesses with access to the much-needed capital. It is a complex process that involves a complex calculation of factors, including creditworthiness, loan amount and terms, and collateral requirements. By understanding the basics of commercial lending, businesses can make informed decisions about their financing needs and position themselves for long-term growth and success.

Chapter 2: Types of Commercial Loans

There are a variety of commercial loans available to borrowers, each with their own unique purposes and requirements. Understanding the different types of commercial loans can help businesses and their lenders choose the best financing option for their needs. In this chapter, we will explore the most common types of commercial loans.

Term Loans

A term loan is a loan that is repaid over a set period, typically ranging from one to ten years. Term loans can be secured or unsecured, and are used to finance a variety of business expenses, such as equipment purchases, expansion, and working capital. Interest rates on term loans can be fixed or variable, and repayment terms can be structured to fit the borrower's cash flow needs.

Lines of Credit

A line of credit is a revolving loan that allows businesses to access funds as needed. Lines of credit are typically used to finance short-term working capital needs, such as inventory purchases or payroll expenses. Interest rates on lines of credit can be fixed or variable, and repayment terms are flexible, with minimum monthly payments required.

SBA Loans

SBA loans are loans that are backed by the U.S. Small Business Administration (SBA). These loans are typically used to finance working capital, existing business purchases for qualified buyers, equipment purchases, and real estate. SBA loans offer longer repayment terms and lower interest rates than traditional commercial loans, making them an attractive financing option for many small businesses.

Commercial Real Estate Loans

Commercial real estate loans are used to finance the purchase or renovation of commercial real estate properties. These loans are usually secured by the property itself, and typically offer lower interest rates and longer repayment terms than other types of commercial loans.

Equipment Financing

Equipment financing is used to finance the purchase or lease of equipment for a business. These loans are typically secured by the equipment itself, and offer flexible repayment terms and low interest rates.

Accounts Receivable Financing

Accounts receivable financing is a form of short-term financing that allows businesses to sell their accounts receivable to a lender in exchange for cash. This type of financing is typically used to improve cash flow and fund short-term working capital needs.

Merchant Cash Advances

Merchant cash advances are a form of financing that allows businesses to receive an advance on their future credit card sales. These loans are typically used to fund short-term working capital needs, and are repaid through a percentage of future credit card sales.

In summary, there are a variety of commercial loans available to borrowers, each with their own unique features and requirements. Understanding the different types of commercial loans can help businesses choose the best financing option for their needs, whether a business needs to finance working capital, purchase equipment, or invest in real estate, there is a commercial loan available to meet their needs.

Chapter 3: Loan Repayment Options

Once you have secured your commercial loan, it is important to understand the repayment terms to ensure that you can repay the loan on time and avoid default. In this chapter, we will explore the different types of loan repayment structures and their features.

Amortization

Amortization is the most common type of loan repayment structure. Under this option, the loan is repaid in equal installments over a set period, typically ranging anywhere from 1 to 20 years. Each payment consists of both principal and interest, with most of the payment going towards interest in the early years of the loan and towards principal in the later years.

Amortization schedules can vary depending on the loan type and lender, but are typically provided to the borrower before the loan is disbursed. By understanding the amortization schedule, borrowers can plan their cash flow and budget accordingly.

Balloon Payments

A balloon payment is a lump sum payment that is due at the end of the loan term, typically after several years of payments. Balloon payments are often used for large loans that would be difficult to repay in equal installments over a shorter period of time.

Balloon payments can be risky for borrowers, as they require a large payment at the end of the loan term, which can be difficult to budget for. In addition, if the borrower is unable to make the balloon payment, they may be forced to refinance the loan or face default and this can be potentially damaging to a company if interest rates are significantly higher than when the original loan was written.

Interest-Only Payments

Interest-only payments are payments that only cover the interest on the loan, with the principal remaining unpaid until the end of the loan term. Interest-only payments are typically used for short-term loans or loans with variable interest rates.

Interest-only payments can be beneficial for borrowers who need to conserve cash flow in the short term, but can also be risky, as the borrower is not making progress towards repaying the principal of the loan.

Accelerated Repayment

Accelerated repayment structures allow borrowers to repay the loan faster than the amortization schedule requires. By making extra payments towards the principal of the loan, borrowers can reduce the total amount of interest paid over the life of the loan and repay the loan faster.

Accelerated repayment can be beneficial for borrowers who have extra cash flow or want to reduce the total cost of the loan.

However, it is important to check with the lender to ensure that there are no prepayment penalties or fees.

Default and Late Payments

If a borrower is unable to make a loan payment on time, they may be subject to late fees and penalties. If the borrower is consistently unable to make payments, they may default on the loan, which can have serious consequences, such as damage to their credit score and legal action by the lender.

In the event a borrower is unable to make a loan payment, it's important to communicate with the lender as soon as possible to discuss options for repayment or modification of the loan terms. Communicate with your bank, they would rather work with you than go through a lengthy and costly legal battle with you.

To sum things up, understanding your loan repayment structure is an essential part of managing businesses financing. By understanding the different repayment structures and their features, borrowers can plan their cash flow and budget effectively, and avoid default or late payments.

Chapter 4: Commercial Lending Terms and Definitions

Commercial lending involves a wide range of terms and definitions that borrowers should understand in order to navigate the loan process effectively. In this chapter, we will explore some of the most common commercial lending terms and their definitions.

Collateral

Collateral is any asset that is used to secure a loan. In commercial lending, collateral can include real estate, equipment, inventory, and other valuable assets. If the borrower defaults on the loan, the lender may seize the collateral as repayment.

Debt-to-Equity Ratio

The debt-to-equity ratio is a measure of a company's financial leverage, calculated by dividing the total liabilities by the shareholder equity. A higher debt-to-equity ratio indicates that a company is using more debt to finance its operations, which can be risky in the long term and affect the borrower's ability to repay more debt.

Interest Rate

The interest rate is the percentage charged by the lender for borrowing the money. In commercial lending, interest rates can be fixed or variable, and may be based on the borrower's creditworthiness, the type of loan, and other factors. Most loans are written using simple interest but some may use compound interest.

> **Simple Interest**: is calculated using the principal of the loan only, it does not charge interest on previous interest.

> **Compound Interest**: is calculated by charging interest on the principal, plus past interest.

Loan-to-Value Ratio

The loan-to-value ratio is a measure of the loan amount compared to the value of the collateral. For example, if a borrower is seeking a $500,000 loan to purchase a property worth $1,000,000, the loan-to-value ratio would be 50%. A higher loan-to-value ratio indicates a higher level of risk for the lender.

Personal Guaranty

Some lenders may require a personal guaranty, a personal guarantee is a promise by an individual to repay a loan if the borrower is unable to make payments. In commercial lending, personal guarantees are often required for small business loans and startup financing as a way to mitigate the risk for the lender.

Prime Rate

The prime rate is the interest rate that commercial banks charge their most creditworthy customers. The prime rate is often used as a benchmark for commercial lending interest rates.

Refinancing

Refinancing is the process of replacing an existing loan with a new loan, often with more favorable terms or a lower interest rate. In commercial lending, refinancing can be used to reduce the total cost of a loan or to free up cash flow for other business expenses.

SBA Loans

SBA loans are loans guaranteed by the U.S. Small Business Administration. These loans are often used by small businesses to finance startup costs, expand operations, or purchase equipment. SBA loans often have more favorable terms and lower interest rates than traditional commercial loans.

Term

The term is the length of time over which the loan is repaid. Commercial loan terms can range from one year to twenty years or more, depending on the type of loan and the borrower's needs.

In summary, understanding commercial lending terms and definitions is crucial for borrowers to navigate the loan process effectively. By understanding these terms, borrowers can negotiate favorable loan terms, manage their cash flow, and avoid default or other issues.

Chapter 5: Collateral and Lending Risks

Collateral is a crucial aspect of commercial lending, as it provides security for the lender in case the borrower defaults on the loan. In this chapter, we will explore how collateral affects lending risk in the borrowing process

Collateral and Lending Risk

Collateral plays a major role in determining the level of risk involved in a commercial loan. Lenders use collateral to mitigate the risk of default and to ensure that they can recover some or all their investment if the borrower fails to repay the loan. The value and quality of the collateral are key factors in determining the risk level of the loan. Having more collateral in the loan can also provide the borrower more favorable loan terms.

Types of Collateral

Collateral can take many forms, including real estate, inventory, equipment, investment accounts, accounts receivable, and other assets that have value. Real estate is often the most common form of collateral in commercial lending as it has a stable value and is often easier to sell. However, other forms of collateral may be used depending on the nature of the borrower's business.

Valuation of Collateral

Valuation of collateral is the process of determining the value of the collateral that is used to secure the loan. This is important for both the lender and the borrower, as it determines the amount of the loan and the level of risk involved. The value of the collateral can fluctuate over time, which can affect the loan's risk level.

Loan-to-Value Ratio and Collateral

The loan-to-value ratio (LTV) is a measure of the loan amount compared to the value of the collateral. A higher LTV indicates a higher level of risk for the lender. Lenders will typically set a maximum LTV for a given type of collateral, depending on their risk appetite.

Mitigating Lending Risk

Lenders can mitigate lending risk by carefully assessing the value and quality of the collateral, setting appropriate LTV ratios, and requiring personal guarantees or other forms of security. Additionally, lenders may conduct due diligence on the borrower's business and financials to assess the likelihood of repayment.

Default and Collateral

In the event of a default, the lender may seize and sell the collateral to recover their investment. The process of liquidating collateral can be time-consuming and costly, and may result in a loss for the lender if the value of the collateral has declined.

Collateral and Loan Terms

Collateral can also affect the terms of a loan, such as the interest rate and repayment schedule. Borrowers with high-quality collateral may be able to negotiate more favorable loan terms, while borrowers with lower-quality collateral may face higher interest rates and shorter repayment periods.

In conclusion, collateral is a key aspect of commercial lending that affects lending risk for both borrowers and lenders. By understanding the role of collateral in commercial lending, borrowers can make informed decisions about their financing needs and lenders can manage their risk effectively. A borrower understanding their options for providing collateral in advance can help then negotiate favorable terms and save money in the long term.

Chapter 6: Credit Scoring and Business Credit Reports

Credit scoring and business credit reports are important tools that lenders use to evaluate the creditworthiness of potential borrowers. In this chapter, we will explore how credit scoring and business credit reports affect commercial lending.

Credit Scoring

Credit scoring is a method that lenders use to evaluate the creditworthiness of a borrower. It involves analyzing various factors, such as payment history, credit utilization, length of credit history, and types of credit used. The resulting credit score is used to determine the level of risk involved in lending to the borrower.

Business Credit Reports

Business credit reports are like personal credit reports, but they focus on the creditworthiness of a business rather than an individual. They contain information about a business's credit history, payment performance, legal filings, and other financial information. Lenders use business credit reports to assess the creditworthiness of a business and to help determine the terms of a loan.

Factors Affecting Credit Scores and Business Credit Reports

Several factors can affect credit scores and business credit reports including payment history, credit utilization, length of credit history, types of credit used, and legal filings such as bankruptcies or liens. Lenders typically use credit scores and business credit reports as part of their due diligence process to assess the risk of lending to a borrower.

Impact of Credit Scores and Business Credit Reports on Commercial Lending

Credit scores and business credit reports have a significant impact on commercial lending. Lenders use these tools to evaluate the creditworthiness of a borrower and to determine the terms of a loan. Borrowers with high credit scores and positive business credit reports may be benefit from lower interest rates and more favorable loan terms, while those with lower scores may face higher rates and more stringent loan requirements.

Improving Credit Scores and Business Credit Reports

Borrowers can take steps to improve their credit scores and business credit reports by paying bills on time, reducing credit card balances, paying down debt and disputing errors on credit reports. Lenders may also offer guidance on how to improve credit scores and business credit reports so be sure to reach out to lenders long before you are needing financing.

Limitations of Credit Scores and Business Credit Reports

While credit scores and business credit reports are valuable tools for assessing creditworthiness, they do not always tell the whole story. These reports will not provide insight into a borrower's current financial situation, and they may not account for factors such as the borrower's reputation or the nature of their business.

Importance of Credit Scoring and Business Credit Reports in Commercial Lending

Overall, credit scoring and business credit reports play a crucial role in commercial lending. They provide lenders with valuable information about a borrower's creditworthiness and help to mitigate lending risk. Borrowers should strive to maintain positive credit scores and business credit reports to increase their chances of obtaining favorable loan terms.

Chapter 7: Understanding Financial Statements and Tax Returns

In the process of commercial lending, financial statements and tax returns are critical documents that provide lenders with insight into a business's financial health and stability. In this chapter, we will explore how lenders use financial statements and tax returns to assess the creditworthiness of a borrower.

Financial statements and tax returns are essential documents that lenders use to evaluate the financial health of a business. These documents provide valuable information about a business's profitability, revenue, expenses, and debts. By analyzing financial statements and tax returns, lenders can assess a business's ability to repay a loan and determine the terms of the loan.

Types of Financial Statements

There are several types of financial statements that lenders typically review, including:

- **Income Statement**: The income statement provides information on a business's revenue and expenses which can be used to calculate the net income or loss.

- **Balance Sheet**: The balance sheet provides information on a business's assets, liabilities, and equity.
- **Cash Flow Statement**: This statement provides information on a business's cash inflows and outflows which can be used to assess a business's liquidity and ability to repay debts.

Types of Tax Returns

Lenders will also review tax returns to assess a business's financial health. The most common types of tax returns that lenders review include:

- **Corporate Income Tax Returns**: These returns provide information on a business's taxable income and tax liability.
- **Personal Income Tax Returns**: These returns provide information on the income and deductions of business owners.
- **Sales Tax Returns**: These returns provide information on a business's sales tax liability.

Analyzing Financial Statements and Tax Returns

Lenders analyze financial statements and tax returns to assess a business's financial health and ability to repay debt. They may look at factors such as revenue trends, profit margins, debt-to-equity ratio, and cash flow. They may also review tax returns to verify the accuracy of financial statements and to assess the borrower's tax compliance.

While financial statements and tax returns are important tools for assessing creditworthiness, they do have limitations. Financial statements may not provide a complete picture of a business's financial health as they do not account for non-financial factors such as the business's reputation or market trends. Tax returns also have limitations as they depict a business' past performance and may not reflect a business's current financial situation.

In summary, financial statements and tax returns are crucial for lenders in the financing process. They provide lenders with valuable information about a business's financial health and stability, which can be used to assess the risk of lending to a borrower and give insight into their ability to repay future debt. Borrowers should ensure that their financial statements and tax returns are accurate and up-to-date to increase their chances of obtaining financing with favorable terms.

Chapter 8: Understanding Important Debt Ratios

This section is to help readers understand important Debt Ratios, with additional information on each ratio and its significance in the commercial lending process.

Debt-to-Equity Ratio

The debt-to-equity ratio is a financial ratio that compares a company's total debt to its shareholders' equity. It is an important indicator of a company's financial health as it measures the extent to which the company relies on debt financing compared to equity financing. A high debt-to-equity ratio indicates that the company has a higher amount of debt relative to equity which can make it more difficult for the company to obtain additional financing in the future.

To calculate the debt-to-equity ratio, you divide the company's total liabilities by its shareholders' equity. For example, if a company has total liabilities of $500,000 and shareholders' equity of $1,000,000, its debt-to-equity ratio would be 0.5.

A low debt-to-equity ratio is favorable as it indicates that the company has a stronger financial position and is not overly reliant on debt financing. A high debt-to-equity ratio, on the other hand, may be a warning sign to lenders that the company may have difficulty repaying its debts and is at a higher risk of defaulting on its loans, especially if economic conditions turn less favorable.

Debt Service Coverage Ratio

The debt service coverage ratio (DSCR) is a financial ratio that measures a company's ability to generate enough cash flow to cover its debt obligations. This ratio is particularly important for lenders as it gives an indication of the company's ability to repay its debts.

To calculate the DSCR, you divide the company's net operating income by its total debt service. Net operating income is calculated by subtracting operating expenses from operating revenue. Total debt service includes all the company's debt payments including principal and interest payments.

A DSCR of at least 1.25 is generally considered a good benchmark for lenders. This means that the company's cash flow can cover its debt payments by 125%. A DSCR below 1 indicates that the company is not generating enough cash flow to cover its debt payments, which can be a warning sign to lenders that the company may have difficulty repaying additional debts.

Current Ratio

The current ratio is a financial ratio that measures a company's short-term liquidity. It indicates the company's ability to pay off its current debts with its current assets. A current liability is a debt that is due within one year, while a current asset is an asset that is expected to be converted into cash within one year.

To calculate the current ratio, you divide the company's current assets by its current liabilities. For example, if a company has current assets of $500,000 and current liabilities of $400,000, its current ratio would be 1.25.

A current ratio of at least 1.2 is generally considered a good benchmark for lenders. This indicates that the company has enough current assets to cover its current liabilities. A current ratio below 1 indicates that the company may have difficulties meeting its short-term obligations, which can be a negative sign to lenders that the company may have difficulty repaying its debts.

Debt-to-Income Ratio

The debt-to-income (DTI) ratio is a financial ratio that measures an individual's or company's debt relative to their income. It is an important indicator of the borrower's ability to repay their debts. Commercial lenders typically look for a DTI of less than 36%.

To calculate the DTI ratio, you divide the borrower's monthly debt payments by their monthly income. For example, if an individual has monthly debt payments of $2,000 and a monthly income of $6,000, their DTI ratio would be 0.33, or 33%.

In conclusion, understanding important debt ratios is crucial for borrowers looking to secure financing for their business ventures. By knowing these ratios, borrowers can assess their own financial health and identify areas where they need to improve. Lenders use these ratios to evaluate the ability of borrowers the repay debt obligations and determine whether they are eligible for financing. By maintaining healthy debt ratios, borrowers can increase their chances of securing financing and growing their businesses.

Chapter 9: Loan Application Process

The loan application process is the initial part of the commercial lending process. It allows borrowers to apply for financing and lenders to evaluate the borrower's creditworthiness and their ability to repay debt. This will help the lenders determine whether to approve the loan. In this chapter, we will discuss the loan application process in detail and explore the steps involved.

Determine Your Financing Needs

Before you begin the loan application process, it is important to determine your financing needs. This includes identifying the amount of funding you require, the purpose of the loan, and the type of loan you need (refer to chapter 2 to review types of commercial loans). You should also consider your ability to repay the loan and the collateral you can provide to secure the loan.

Gather Your Financial Information

Once you have determined your financing needs, you will need to gather your financial information. This includes your financial statements, tax returns, business plan, and other relevant documents requested by the borrower's lender. You should also be prepared to provide information on your personal and business credit history, as well as any outstanding debts or obligations.

Submit Your Loan Application

Before submitting your loan application, it is important to research potential lenders and find those that offer the type of loan you need. You should consider the lender's reputation, interest rates, fees, and repayment terms. You may also want to consider working directly with a lender or a consultant who can help you identify lenders and negotiate loan terms on your behalf.

Once you have gathered your financial information and researched potential lenders you can submit your loan application. Most lenders will require you to complete an application form and provide supporting documentation. Some lenders may require you to pay an application fee.

After submitting your loan application, you will need to wait for the lender to review your application and determine whether to approve the loan. This process can take several weeks or even months depending on the lender's policies and the complexity of your loan request.

When evaluating a loan application, lenders consider several factors, including:

1. Credit score: A borrower's credit score is a measure of their creditworthiness and their ability to repay debt. Lenders typically require a minimum credit score for loan approval.
2. Financial statements: A borrower's financial statements provide a snapshot of their financial health, including their income, expenses, assets, and liabilities.
3. Collateral: Collateral is an asset that a borrower pledges to secure a loan. Lenders may require collateral to reduce their risk of loss in the event of default.
4. Debt-to-income ratio: A borrower's debt-to-income ratio is a measure of their debt obligations relative to their income.

Lenders use this ratio to assess a borrower's ability to repay the loan.

5. Business plan: A borrower's business plan provides a detailed description of their business, including their goals, strategies, and financial projections.

Negotiate Loan Terms

If your loan application is approved, the lender will provide you with a loan offer that outlines the loan terms, including the interest rate, repayment schedule, and any fees or charges associated with the loan. You should review these terms carefully and negotiate any terms that you feel are unfavorable. It is encouraged to have multiple lenders working on your loan at the same time to give you options when making your decision and to help give you leverage while negotiating with other lenders.

Close the Loan

Once you have negotiated the loan terms and are satisfied with the offer, the time has come to close the loan. This involves signing the loan agreement and providing any required collateral or security. The lender will then disburse the loan funds to your account.

Loan Funding

Loan funding is the process by which a lender disburses the loan funds to the borrower. Once a loan has been approved, the lender will provide the borrower with a loan agreement that outlines the terms of the loan, including the interest rate, repayment schedule, and any fees or charges associated with the loan.

The borrower will need to sign the loan agreement and provide any required collateral or security before the lender can disburse the loan funds. The loan funds may be disbursed in a lump sum or in installments, depending on the loan agreement.

Factors Considered in Loan Funding

When disbursing loan funds, lenders consider several factors, including:

1. Loan disbursement schedule: The loan disbursement schedule outlines when and how the loan funds will be disbursed.
2. Collateral: If collateral is required, the lender will need to verify the value of the collateral before disbursing the loan funds.
3. Loan documentation: The lender will need to verify that all loan documentation is complete and accurate before disbursing funds.
4. Loan conditions: If any conditions were imposed on the loan approval, such as the completion of certain tasks or the provision of additional documentation, the lender will need to verify that these conditions have been met before disbursement.

The loan application process can be complex and time-consuming, but it is an essential part of raising capital. By following the steps outlined in this chapter and working with a trusted lender or loan broker, you can increase your chances of success and obtain the financing you need to achieve your business goals.

Chapter 10: Business Lines of Credit

A business line of credit is a type of commercial loan that provides a flexible source of financing for businesses to use for multiple needs. In this chapter, we will explore the basics of revolving lines of credit, not limited to how they work, their benefits and drawbacks, and how to obtain them.

What is a Business Line of Credit

A business line of credit is a revolving loan that allows a borrower to access funds up to a predetermined credit limit. The borrower can draw funds as needed and only pay interest on the amount borrowed. Once the borrower repays the borrowed funds, they become available again for future use.

Unlike a term loan, which provides a lump sum of money that is repaid over a set period, a business line of credit provides ongoing access to funds. This arrangement makes it a flexible financing option that can be used for a variety of business needs such as covering short-term cash flow gaps, purchasing inventory, payroll, or financing growth opportunities.

Benefits of a Business Line of Credit

Revolving lines of credit have several benefits, including:

1.Flexibility: A business line of credit provides ongoing access to funds that can be used as needed. This makes it a flexible financing option that can adapt to changing business needs.

2.Cost-effective: Borrowers only pay interest on the amount borrowed making business lines of credit a cost-effective financing option.

3.Improving credit: Consistently paying back a business line of credit can help improve a borrower's credit score, making it easier to obtain financing in the future.

4.Fast access to funds: Once a business line of credit has been approved, funds can be accessed quickly and easily, providing businesses with the cash they need to cover unexpected expenses or take advantage of growth opportunities.

Drawbacks of a Business Line of Credit

There can also be drawbacks to using a business line of credit, including:

1. High-interest rates: Business lines of credit tend to have higher interest rates than other forms of financing, which result in increased financing costs.

2. Collateral: Many business lines of credit require collateral to secure the loan, which can be difficult for businesses that are unable to meet the collateral requirements.

3. Fees: Some lenders may charge fees for using a business line of credit, such as annual fees, maintenance fees, or transaction fees.

How to Obtain a Business Line of Credit

To obtain a business line of credit, a borrower will need to meet certain requirements, including:

1. Good credit: Lenders will typically require a minimum credit score for approval, and a borrower's credit history will be closely scrutinized.
2. Financial Statements: Lenders will review a borrower's financial statements, including income statements and balance sheets, to assess their financial health.
3. Business plan: Lenders will want to see a borrower's business plan, including their goals, strategies, and financial projections.
4. Collateral: Many lenders require collateral to secure a business line of credit, which can be in the form of inventory, accounts receivable, or real estate.
5. Cash flow: Lenders will want to see evidence of positive cash flow and a steady revenue stream to ensure that the borrower will be able to repay the loan.

Business lines of credit are a flexible and cost-effective financing option for businesses. By understanding the benefits and drawbacks of a business line of credit, and the requirements for obtaining one, businesses can determine whether it is the right financing option for their needs. It is important to work with a trusted lender or loan broker who can provide guidance and support throughout the process of obtaining a business line of credit.

Chapter 11: Business Lines of Credit

Small Business Administration (SBA) Loans

The Small Business Administration (SBA) is a federal agency that provides support and resources to small businesses in the United States. One of the key programs offered by the SBA is its loan program which provides access to capital for small businesses that might not otherwise qualify for traditional commercial loans. In this chapter, we will explore the basics of SBA loans, including their benefits and drawbacks, and how to obtain them.

Let us begin with, what is an SBA Loan? An SBA loan is a type of government-backed loan that is designed to help small businesses access affordable financing. The SBA does not provide loans directly to borrowers; instead, it partners with participating lenders to provide guarantees for loans made to small businesses.

SBA loans can be used for a variety of business purposes, including working capital, real estate purchases, equipment purchases, and business acquisitions. The loan terms, including interest rates and repayment periods, are set by the lender, but the SBA provides guidelines for the maximum loan amounts and interest rates that lenders can charge.

Benefits of SBA Loans

There are several benefits to choosing an SBA loan, including:

1. Lower interest rates: SBA loans typically offer lower interest rates than other commercial loans making them a more affordable financing option for small businesses.
2. Longer repayment terms: SBA loans can have longer repayment terms than other commercial loans which can make the monthly payments more manageable for small businesses.
3. Easier to qualify: Because SBA loans are government-backed, lenders may be more willing to lend to small businesses that might not qualify for traditional commercial loans.
4. Flexible use of funds: SBA loans can be used for a variety of business purposes giving small businesses the flexibility to use the funds as needed.

Drawbacks of SBA Loans

There are a few drawbacks to using an SBA loan, including:

1. Lengthy application process: The application process for an SBA loan can be lengthy and time-consuming, requiring extensive documentation and financial statements.
2. Collateral requirements: SBA loans may require collateral to secure the loan, which can be difficult for small businesses that do not have significant assets.
3. Strict eligibility requirements: SBA loans have strict eligibility requirements, including a minimum credit score and proof of the ability to repay the loan.
4. Limited loan amounts: SBA loans have maximum loan amounts, which may not be sufficient for some small businesses' financing needs.

How to Obtain an SBA Loan

To obtain an SBA loan, a borrower will need to follow a specific application process, including:

1. Determine eligibility: Small businesses must meet certain eligibility requirements, including being a for-profit business operating in the United States, and meeting the SBA's size standards.
2. Gather documentation: Lenders will require extensive documentation, including business and personal financial statements, tax returns, and business plans.
3. Choose a lender: Small businesses can choose from a variety of SBA-approved lenders, including banks, credit unions, and online lenders.
4. Submit the application: Once all documentation is gathered, the borrower will need to submit the loan application to the chosen lender.
5. Wait for approval: The lender will review the application and decide on whether to approve the loan. If approved, the borrower will need to sign loan documents and provide collateral.

SBA loans can be a valuable source of affordable financing for small businesses. By understanding the benefits and drawbacks of SBA loans and the application process, small businesses can determine whether an SBA loan is the right financing option for their needs. It is important to work with a trusted lender or loan broker who can provide guidance and support throughout the process of obtaining an SBA loan.

Chapter 12: Asset-Based Loans

Asset-based lending (ABL) is a type of commercial lending that uses a borrower's assets, such as inventory, accounts receivable, and equipment as collateral for a loan. Asset-Based-Lending provides financing to businesses that may not qualify for traditional commercial loans due to a lack of credit history, poor financial statements, or other reasons. In this chapter we will explore the basics of asset-based lending, including its benefits and drawbacks, and how it can be used to finance a business.

Asset-based lending is a form of commercial lending that uses a company's assets as collateral for a loan. The collateral provides security for the lender and helps to mitigate the risk associated with lending to a business. The assets used as collateral can include:

1. Inventory: The value of a company's inventory can be used as collateral for an ABL loan.
2. Accounts receivable: The outstanding payments due from a company's customers can be used as collateral for an ABL loan.
3. Equipment: The value of a company's equipment can be used as collateral for an ABL loan.

Lenders that have issued asset-based-loans typically conduct regular inspections of the collateral to ensure that it is being properly managed and maintained. In the event of default, the lender has the right to take possession of the collateral and sell it to recoup the outstanding loan balance.

Benefits of Asset-Based Loans

There are several benefits to using asset-based loans, including:

1. Increased borrowing capacity: Asset-Based-Loans can provide businesses with a higher borrowing capacity than traditional commercial loans as the collateral allows lenders to take on more risk.
2. Flexible use of funds: Asset-Based-Loans can be used for a variety of business purposes, including working capital, inventory purchases, and capital expenditures.
3. Quicker access to funds: Asset-Based-Loans can be processed quicker than traditional commercial loans as the collateral provides a level of security for the lender.
4. Improved cash flow: By using accounts receivable as collateral, businesses can turn their outstanding payments into immediate cash which can improve their cash flow and help them to manage their finances more effectively.

Downsides of Asset-Based Loans

There are also some drawbacks to using asset-based lending, including:

1. Higher interest rates: Asset-Based-Loans typically have higher interest rates than traditional commercial loans as the collateral does not always provide sufficient security to offset the risk of lending to the borrower.
2. Strict collateral requirements: Lenders that issue asset-based-loans may have strict collateral requirements which can limit the types of assets that can be used as collateral.

3. Ongoing collateral management: Lenders may require regular inspections of the collateral to ensure that it is being properly managed and maintained.
4. Risk of default: If a borrower defaults on an asset-based-loan, the lender has the right to take possession of the collateral and sell it to recoup the outstanding loan balance. This can have significant implications for the borrower's future business operations.

How to Obtain Asset-Based Loans

In order to obtain asset-based loans, a borrower will need to follow an application process similar to other lending programs, including:

1. Determine eligibility: A borrower must determine whether they have sufficient assets to use as collateral for an ABL loan.
2. Gather documentation: ABL lenders will require extensive documentation, including financial statements, accounts receivable aging reports, and inventory reports.
3. Submit the application: Once all documentation is gathered, the borrower will need to submit the loan application to the chosen lender.
4. Wait for approval: The lender will review the application and decide on whether to approve the loan. If approved, the borrower will need to sign
5. Manage collateral: Once the loan is approved, the borrower will need to manage the collateral according to the lender's requirements. This may include regular inspections of inventory and accounts receivable, as well as ongoing reporting to the lender.
6. Repay the loan: The borrower will need to make regular payments on the loan, typically on a monthly basis. Failure to make payments can result in default and the lender may take possession of the collateral.

Types of Asset-Based Loans

There are several types of asset-based loans, each with their own unique characteristics and requirements.

1. Traditional asset-based loan: This type of loan is offered by banks and other traditional lenders. It typically requires collateral in the form of accounts receivable, inventory, and equipment.
2. Trade finance: This type of loan is used to finance international trade transactions. The collateral is typically the goods being shipped, and the loan is repaid once the goods are sold.
3. Factoring: Factoring is a type of loan that involves the sale of accounts receivable to a third-party (known as a factor) at a discount. The factor takes ownership of the receivables and collects the outstanding payments from customers.
4. Equipment financing: This type of asset loan is used to finance the purchase of equipment. The equipment itself serves as collateral for the loan.

Asset-based loans can be an effective way for businesses to obtain financing when traditional commercial loans are not available or do not meet their needs. By using assets such as inventory, accounts receivable, and equipment as collateral, businesses can increase their borrowing capacity, obtain flexible use of funds, and improve their cash flow. On the other side, asset-based loans also come with higher interest rates, strict collateral requirements, ongoing collateral management, and the risk of default if these factors are not managed properly. It is important for borrowers to carefully consider the benefits and drawbacks of asset-based loans before deciding if it is the right financing option for their business.

Chapter 13: Equipment Financing

Equipment financing is a type of commercial loan that allows businesses to purchase equipment needed for their operations. This type of financing is commonly used by businesses in various industries, including manufacturing, transportation, construction, and healthcare.

Equipment financing involves a lender providing a loan or lease to a business for the purchase of equipment with the equipment itself serving as collateral for the loan. In this chapter, we will explore the benefits and drawbacks of equipment financing, the types of equipment that can be financed, and the steps involved in obtaining equipment financing.

Benefits of Equipment Financing

1. Preserves working capital: Equipment financing allows businesses to acquire equipment without having to pay for it all at once preserving their working capital for other business expenses.
2. Fixed payments: Equipment financing typically involves fixed monthly payments, which can help businesses budget more effectively.

3. Tax benefits: Equipment financing can provide tax benefits, such as the ability to deduct the interest and depreciation expenses on equipment purchases.
4. Provides Up-to-date equipment: Equipment financing allows businesses to keep their equipment up to date without having to make large capital expenditures providing them the ability to be more efficient and productive in their work.
5. Preserves credit lines: Equipment financing does not use up credit lines, which can be important for businesses that may need to access credit in the future.

Types of Equipment Financing

1. Equipment Loans: Equipment loans are a type of secured loan that allows businesses to borrow money to purchase equipment. The equipment serves as collateral for the loan, and the loan is typically repaid over a period of 1-7 years.
2. Equipment Leases: Equipment leases allow businesses to use equipment for a fixed period of time in exchange for regular lease payments. At the end of the lease term, the business may have the option to purchase the equipment, return it, or renew the lease.
3. Sale-Leaseback Financing: Sale-leaseback financing involves a business selling equipment it already owns to a lender and then leasing it back. This allows the business to receive cash from the sale of the equipment while still being able to use it.
4. Equipment Rental: Equipment rental involves a business renting equipment for a short period of time, usually on a daily or weekly basis.

Steps to Obtaining Equipment Financing

1. Determine the type of equipment needed: The first step in obtaining equipment financing is to determine the type of equipment needed, its estimated cost and how long you will need the equipment.

2. Research lenders: Businesses should research potential lenders to find one that offers equipment financing that meets their needs.

3. Gather financial information: Lenders will require financial information from the business, such as income statements, balance sheets, and tax returns.

4. Choose the type of financing: Businesses should choose the type of equipment financing that best fits their needs, whether it be a loan, lease, sale-leaseback financing, or equipment rental.

5. Apply for financing: Businesses should complete the lender's application process, which may include providing a detailed description of the equipment to be financed, the estimated cost, and the expected useful life of the equipment.

6. Receive funds: Once approved, the lender will provide the funds needed to purchase the equipment.

Equipment financing can be an attractive option for businesses that need to purchase equipment but do not want to pay for it all at up front. By using the equipment, itself as collateral, businesses can obtain financing with fixed payments, tax benefits, and the ability to keep their working capital and credit lines intact. However, equipment financing also comes with risks, such as the risk of default and the requirement to maintain the equipment in good working order. It is important for businesses to carefully consider the benefits and drawbacks of equipment financing before deciding if it is the right financing option for their needs.

Chapter 14: Real Estate Financing

Real estate loans are loans used to purchase real estate for commercial or personal use. In this chapter, we will explore the different types of loans used to purchase real estate as well as the benefits and drawbacks of each, and the steps involved in obtaining real estate financing.

Types of Real Estate Financing

1. Commercial Loans: Commercial loans are used to purchase commercial properties, such as office buildings, warehouses, or retail spaces. The property serves as collateral for the loan, and the loan is typically repaid over a period of 10-30 years.
2. Residential Mortgages: Residential mortgages are used to purchase residential properties, such as single-family homes, townhouses, or condominiums. The property serves as collateral for the loan, and the loan is typically repaid over a period of 15-30 years.
3. Construction Loans: Construction loans are used to finance the construction of a new building or the renovation of an existing building. The loan is typically repaid once the construction is complete, or the borrower may refinance with a long-term mortgage.

4. Bridge Loans: Bridge loans are used to provide short-term financing for real estate transactions, typically used when the borrower needs to close on a property quickly, but may not have the funds available yet. The loan is typically repaid once the borrower obtains long-term financing, or the property is sold.

Benefits and Drawbacks of Real Estate Financing

1. Long-term financing: Real estate financing can provide long-term financing for large purchases allowing borrowers to spread out payments over several years.
2. Fixed interest rates: Many real estate financing options offer fixed interest rates, allowing borrowers to budget more effectively and avoid unexpected rate increases.
3. Building equity: As borrowers make payments on their real estate financing, they build equity in their property, which can be used for future financing needs.
4. Collateral: Real estate serves as collateral for the loan, which can make it easier to obtain financing.
5. Down payments: Real estate financing typically requires a significant down payment, which can be a challenge for some borrowers.
6. Risk of default: Real estate financing carries a risk of default, which can result in the borrower losing the property and damaging their credit score.

Steps to Obtain Real Estate Financing

1. Determine your financing needs: Before applying for real estate financing, determine how much you need to borrow and for what purpose.
2. Choose a lender: Research lenders that offer the type of real estate financing you need and compare their rates and terms.
3. Gather documentation: Lenders will require documentation, such as financial statements, tax returns, and credit reports, to assess your eligibility for real estate financing.

4. Submit an application: Complete the lender's application process, providing all required documentation and information.
5. Wait for approval: The lender will review your application and determine whether to approve or deny your request for financing.
6. Close the loan: If approved, you will need to sign a loan agreement and complete any other closing requirements, such as obtaining title insurance.

Real estate financing can be a valuable tool for businesses and individuals looking to purchase real estate. By understanding the different types of real estate financing, the benefits and drawbacks of each, and the steps involved in obtaining financing, borrowers can make informed decisions about their real estate financing needs.

Chapter 15: Multifamily Financing

Multifamily properties, such as apartment buildings and condominiums, can be a profitable investment for property owners. However, purchasing and financing multifamily properties can be complex. In this chapter, we will explore the process of obtaining a loan for multifamily properties, including the requirements, types of loans, and tips for success.

Requirements for Multifamily Property Loans

1. Credit Score: Borrowers will need a good credit score to obtain a loan for a multifamily property. A credit score of 680 or higher is typically required.
2. Debt-to-Income Ratio: Lenders will look at a borrower's debt-to-income ratio to determine their ability to repay the loan. A ratio of 45% or less is typically required.
3. Down Payment: Borrowers will need to provide a significant down payment to obtain a loan for a multifamily property. The down payment can range from 15-30% of the property's value. This can vary based off purchase price and loan program.
4. Property Appraisal: Lenders will require an appraisal of the property to determine its value and ensure that it meets their lending criteria.

5. Property Management Experience: Borrowers who have experience managing multifamily properties are more likely to be approved for a loan. You may also want to consider using a property management company and including this plan in your proposal to the lender.

Types of Loans for Multifamily Properties

1. Conventional Loans: Conventional loans are traditional loans offered by banks and other lenders. These loans typically have lower interest rates and longer repayment terms than other loan options.
2. Federal Housing Administration (FHA) loans: FHA loans are government-backed loans that are available to borrowers with lower credit scores and smaller down payments than conventional loans. However, FHA loans may have higher interest rates and stricter eligibility requirements.
3. Veterans Affairs (VA) loans: VA loans are available to eligible veterans and their families and offer competitive interest rates and flexible repayment terms.
4. Private Loans: Private loans are loans offered by private lenders and may have higher interest rates and shorter repayment terms than other loan options.

Tips for Success in Obtaining a Loan for Multifamily Properties

1. Work with a knowledgeable lender: Choose a lender who has experience in financing multifamily properties and can guide you through the process.
2. Build relationships with lenders: Building relationships with lenders can help you secure financing for future investments.
3. Have a solid business plan: Develop a solid business plan that outlines your investment strategy, financial projections, and management approach.

4. Be prepared to provide documentation: Lenders will require documentation, such as financial statements, tax returns, and property appraisals, to assess your eligibility for financing.
5. Consider partnering with others: Partnering with other investors or property managers can help you secure financing and manage the property more effectively. This is especially good advice when you are first starting out.

Obtaining a loan for a multifamily property can be a complex process, but with the right knowledge and preparation borrowers can successfully secure financing for their investment. By understanding the requirements for multifamily property loans, the types of loans available, and tips for success, borrowers can make informed decisions and maximize their chances of securing financing for their multifamily property investment.

Chapter 16: Obtaining A Loan with Multiple Investors

When obtaining a commercial loan, it is not uncommon for multiple investors to come together to finance a project. This can be an effective way to share the financial risk and take on larger projects. However, obtaining a commercial loan with multiple investors can be complex. In this chapter, we will explore the process of obtaining a commercial loan with multiple investors, including the requirements and documents needed.

Requirements for Obtaining a Commercial Loan with Multiple Investors

1. Credit Score: Each investor will need to have a good credit score to qualify for the loan. Typically, a credit score of 680 or higher is required.
2. Debt-to-Income Ratio: Lenders will look at each investor's debt-to-income ratio to determine their ability to repay the loan. A ratio of 45% or less is typically required.

3. Down Payment: Each investor will need to provide a portion of the down payment for the loan. The exact amount will depend on the loan and the lender's requirements as well as the operating agreement between the investors.
4. Business Plan: A comprehensive business plan will be required that outlines the investment strategy, financial projections, and management approach.
5. Legal Documents: Each investor will need to provide legal documents that detail their ownership and financial contributions to the project.

Required Documents

1. Articles of Incorporation: If the project is being funded through a corporation, the articles of incorporation will need to be provided.
2. Operating Agreement: If the project is being funded through a limited liability company (LLC), an operating agreement will need to be provided.
3. Financial Statements: Each investor will need to provide financial statements, including tax returns and bank statements, to demonstrate their financial health and ability to repay the loan.
4. Loan Application: The loan application will need to include the financial details of the project, including the loan amount, repayment terms, and interest rate.
5. Legal documents: Each investor will need to provide legal documents that detail their ownership and financial contributions to the project.

Tips for Success

1. Work with a knowledgeable lender: Choose a lender who has experience in financing projects with multiple investors and can guide you through the process.
2. Build strong relationships with multiple investors: Building strong relationships with investors can help you secure

financing for future projects and expand your investment portfolio.

3. Develop a solid business plan: Develop a comprehensive business plan that outlines your investment strategy, financial projections, and management approach.

4. Communicate effectively with all investors: Effective communication is crucial when working with multiple investors. Keep all investors informed about the project's progress and any changes in the financial or management plan.

5. Be prepared to provide documentation: Lenders will require extensive documentation to assess the eligibility of each investor and ensure the project's financial viability.

Obtaining a commercial loan with multiple investors can be complex, but it can also be an effective way to finance larger projects and share financial risk. By understanding the requirements for obtaining a commercial loan with multiple investors and the documents needed, investors can make informed decisions and maximize their chances of securing financing for their project. By working with a knowledgeable lender, building strong relationships with investors, developing a solid business plan, communicating effectively, and being prepared to provide documentation, investors can successfully navigate the loan process and achieve their investment goals.

Conclusion

I hope this book left you with a better basic understanding of the Commercial Lending process. Obtaining commercial financing is an important decision in any business's life cycle, no matter how large or small. It is important to work with a knowledgeable bank and lender as well as understand the process yourself in order to make the process run smoothly and efficiently.

Make sure you work with experienced lenders and shop around for rates and terms. Setting up your business up with favorable terms and a lending plan can be the difference between your business sticking around for years to come or ending as quickly as it started. Be sure to follow your business plan and stick to your lending terms and you will give yourself the best chance of success.

Printed in Great Britain
by Amazon

38305040R00036